Tahiti

A Tourist Encyclopedia

Mark M Karl

Table of content

Chapter 7
Practical Tips and Safety

A wine store in Tahiti

Chapter 1

Introduction to Tahiti

Background information about Tahiti's history, culture, and geography:

Tahiti, situated in the South Pacific Ocean, is the biggest and most populated island in French Polynesia. It is part of an archipelago of 118 islands and atolls, recognized for their spectacular beauty, blue seas, and teeming marine life. Tahiti maintains a major position in history and has a rich cultural legacy.

History: Tahiti's history extends back thousands of years when it was initially populated by Polynesians who moved from Southeast Asia. These early residents formed a distinct culture and civilization, which flourished in isolation until the advent of European explorers.

The first European encounter with Tahiti happened in 1767 when British explorer Samuel

Wallis spotted the island. Subsequently, French navigator Louis-Antoine de Bougainville reached Tahiti in 1768, followed by Captain James Cook in 1769. These meetings with European explorers marked the beginning of European influence in the area.

During the 19th century, missionaries from Europe came to Tahiti, resulting in the conversion of the majority of the inhabitants to Christianity. In 1842, Tahiti became a French protectorate, and later in 1880, it was fully acquired by France. French influence has had a lasting effect on the culture, language, and administration of the islands.

Culture: Tahitian culture is strongly entrenched in Polynesian traditions, typified by a strong connection to nature, music, dance, and oral storytelling. The traditional Tahitian society was structured into hierarchical social systems, with chiefs (ari'i) holding political authority and religious leaders (to'ohu) responsible for spiritual affairs.

The arts, notably music, and dancing, play a vital role in Tahitian culture. Traditional musical instruments, including the ukulele, drums, and conch shells, are utilized to generate rhythmic tunes accompanying the energetic dances. The most renowned type of Tahitian dance is the 'ote'a, characterized by fast hip motions and intense performances.

Tahitian mythology and folklore focus on gods and goddesses, notably the creator deity Ta'aroa and the goddess of beauty and fertility, Hina. These tales and legends are typically reproduced in wood carvings, tapa cloth paintings, and other kinds of traditional artwork.

Geography: Tahiti consists of two major islands: Tahiti Nui (meaning "big Tahiti") and Tahiti Iti (meaning "small Tahiti"). Tahiti Nui is the bigger of the two and is marked by towering volcanic peaks, notably Mount Orohena, the highest point in French Polynesia. Tahiti Iti is a peninsula situated in the southeastern section of the island

and is recognized for its rough coastline and scenic beaches.

The islands are bordered by spectacular coral reefs and lagoons, which form a complex environment sustaining a variety of marine life. The vivid underwater environment of Tahiti draws snorkelers and scuba divers from throughout the globe.

Introduction to the local language, traditions, and etiquette:
The official languages of French Polynesia, including Tahiti, are French and Tahitian. Tahitian, an Austronesian language, is extensively spoken among the local people and represents the cultural legacy of the islands.

When dealing with the natives, it is helpful to acquire a few Tahitian pleasantries and phrases. Common greetings include "Ia ora na" (hello) and "Nana" (goodbye). Respect for the culture is crucial, and tourists should make an effort to learn about local traditions and obey cultural conventions.

Tahitians revere their traditions and practices, notably the practice of fa'a'apu (sharing and mutual respect) and the notion of 'aita pea pea (laid-back attitude). It is traditional to show respect for elders and have a warm and easygoing manner while talking with natives.

Etiquette in Tahiti encompasses behaviors such as removing shoes before entering houses or holy locations, dressing modestly while visiting churches or religious sites, and asking for permission before taking pictures of persons or cultural activities.

Understanding and understanding the local language, traditions, and etiquette may enrich the whole vacation experience in Tahiti and develop important ties with the people and the culture of the islands.

Chapter 2

Planning Your Trip

Best time to visit Tahiti and considerations for various seasons:

Tahiti offers a tropical environment throughout the year, making it an attractive destination for beach lovers and outdoor enthusiasts. However, there are several variables to bear in mind while organizing the scheduling of your vacation.

peak Season (May to October): This time is called the peak season in Tahiti because of the cooler and dryer weather. The temperatures vary from the mid-70s°F (mid-20s°C) to the mid-80s°F (about 30°C). The sky is normally clear, and rainfall is less common. It is a good season for aquatic sports such as snorkeling, diving, and sailing. However, bear in mind that this is also the peak tourist season, so popular sights and lodgings may be more crowded, and costs may be higher.

Shoulder Season (April and November): The months of April and November are considered the shoulder seasons in Tahiti. The weather at this time is often good, with fewer people compared to the busy season. It's a perfect time to enjoy outdoor activities while taking advantage of discounted lodging costs. However, it's crucial to know that there may be occasional showers and a little rise in humidity throughout these months.

Low Season (December to March): The low season in Tahiti correlates to the wetter and warmer months. The temperatures vary from the upper 70s°F (about 25°C) to the mid-80s°F (approximately 30°C). While rainfall is more common, it normally happens in short spurts, giving opportunities for recreational activities in between showers. The low season gives the chance to discover Tahiti with fewer people and more inexpensive costs for lodgings and flights. However, it's worth mentioning that certain water activities may be hindered owing to weather conditions.

Entry criteria, visas, and travel documents:

Passport: All travelers to Tahiti must have a valid passport. Ensure that your passport has at least six months of validity beyond your scheduled departure date.

Visas: Depending on your nationality, you may require a visa to visit Tahiti. For citizens of numerous countries, including the United States, Canada, the European Union, Australia, and New Zealand, a visa is not needed for visits of up to 90 days. However, it's crucial to examine the precise visa requirements depending on your nationality before flying.

Return Ticket: It is important to have a return or onward ticket to prove your intention to depart Tahiti within the specified time range.

Proof of lodging: It's suggested to have proof of your lodging reservations for the length of your stay.

Customs and Immigration: Upon arriving in Tahiti, you will need to undergo customs and immigration formalities. Be prepared to provide your passport, completed arrival card, and any relevant travel documentation.

Tips for discovering acceptable lodgings and deciding between resorts, hotels, or vacation rentals:

Resorts: Tahiti is recognized for its magnificent resorts, which provide gorgeous overwater bungalows and superb services. Resorts typically include a variety of amenities, including restaurants, pools, spas, and water sports facilities. They are great for guests wanting a luxurious and all-inclusive experience. However, bear in mind that resorts might be more costly compared to other hotel alternatives.

Hotels: There are different hotels accessible in Tahiti, ranging from boutique businesses to worldwide famous brands. Hotels provide pleasant lodgings with facilities such as restaurants, swimming pools, and concierge services. They are perfect for tourists searching for ease, comfort, and a diversity of services to meet various budgets.

Vacation Rentals: Renting a vacation house or villa may be a terrific alternative for families or bigger parties. Vacation rentals give additional room and privacy and frequently come equipped with kitchens or kitchenettes, allowing guests self-catering. They may be found in numerous places around the islands, including seaside houses and remote spots. Vacation rentals provide a more autonomous and immersive experience in Tahiti.

When picking lodgings in Tahiti, consider criteria such as location, accessibility to attractions and activities, facilities, budget, and personal preferences. It's recommended to study and compare alternatives, read reviews, and book in advance, especially during the busy season, to obtain the greatest pricing and availability.

Chapter 3

Getting to Tahiti

Overview of the various transportation choices, including aircraft and cruises:

Flights: The principal means of transportation for reaching Tahiti is flying. The principal international gateway is Faa'a International Airport (PPT), situated in the capital city of Papeete on the island of Tahiti. Several major airlines provide frequent flights to Tahiti from international locations such as Los Angeles, Paris, Auckland, and Sydney. Additionally, there are internal flights linking Tahiti with other islands within French Polynesia, offering quick access to diverse places.

Cruises: Another popular method to visit Tahiti is via cruises. Many cruise companies offer itineraries that visit Tahiti and other islands in the area. Cruises give a unique chance to tour various islands, see the beautiful grandeur of the

South Pacific, and enjoy onboard facilities and entertainment. The major port for cruise ships in Tahiti is Papeete Harbor, and different cruise choices are available, ranging from luxury cruises to more budget-friendly ones.

Tips for booking flights and discovering the most convenient routes:

Research and Compare: Before booking your tickets to Tahiti, undertake comprehensive research and compare costs, itineraries, and airlines. Use internet travel agents, airline websites, and flight comparison websites to discover the greatest bargains. Consider flexibility in travel dates and be open to alternate departure and arrival airports to discover the most convenient and cost-effective possibilities.

Timing: Booking flights long in advance is often suggested to obtain better costs and availability, particularly during the busy season. However, some last-minute offers may be available, so it's worth checking for any savings closer to your vacation dates. Be conscious of any seasonal pricing swings and prepare appropriately.

Stopovers: Depending on your departure location, you may have the option of picking flights with stopovers. Stopovers might be a chance to break up a lengthy drive and discover another place along the route. Consider the length of the stopover, since longer layovers might give a chance for a brief visit or an overnight stay.

Airlines: Research several airlines that conduct flights to Tahiti and read reviews to determine their service quality and dependability. Some prominent airlines that travel to Tahiti are Air Tahiti Nui, Air France, Air New Zealand, Hawaiian Airlines, and Qantas. Pay attention to luggage limitations, onboard facilities, and any extra expenses to make an educated selection.

Information about local transportation inside the islands, such as taxis, rental automobiles, and public transit:

Taxis: Taxis are accessible on the major islands of Tahiti, Moorea, and Bora Bora. In Tahiti, cabs may be obtained at the airport, near hotels, and in the major cities. It's essential to negotiate the fee before commencing the ride or guarantee the driver utilizes the meter. Taxis are metered, and extra costs may apply for late-night or out-of-town travels. In more isolated places, it's advised to prearrange transportation or ask about your lodging.

Rental Cars: Renting a vehicle is a great method to tour the islands alone. Car rental businesses may be located at airports, large cities, and certain resorts. Driving is on the right side of the road in French Polynesia. It's crucial to have a valid driver's license, be aware of local driving rules, and use care on narrow or curving roads. Booking in advance is essential, particularly during high seasons, to assure availability.

Public transit: On the larger islands, such as Tahiti and Moorea, there are local bus services that offer transit between towns and famous tourist locations. Buses are an economical choice, although timetables may be restricted, particularly on weekends and holidays. It's essential to check the schedules in advance and be prepared for unexpected delays. Additionally, on certain islands, bicycles, scooters, and electric bikes may be hired for exploration at a leisurely pace.

Ferries: Inter-island ferries run between Tahiti and other adjacent islands, giving an additional way of transportation. Ferry services are offered to places like Moorea, Huahine, Raiatea, and Bora Bora. Schedules and availability may change, therefore it's advisable to check in advance and buy tickets for local transportation within the islands, consider issues such as the distance to be travelled, the amount of flexibility needed, and the particular sites and activities to be visited. Different types of transportation may be utilised to maximize your trip experience in French Polynesia.

Chapter 4

Exploring Tahiti's Natural Beauty

Tahiti, the biggest island in French Polynesia, is famed for its stunning beaches, captivating lagoons, and brilliant coral reefs. Its natural beauty is unsurpassed, making it a paradise for beach lovers and water aficionados from across the globe. Let's begin on a thorough tour around Tahiti's magnificent landscapes and enjoy the vast selection of water sports and natural marvels it has to offer.

The beaches of Tahiti are nothing short of awe-inspiring. Imagine powdery white dunes reaching as far as the eye can see, meeting the crystal-clear turquoise seas of the South Pacific Ocean. One such notable beach is Matira Beach, situated on the island of Bora Bora, only a short flight or boat ride away from Tahiti. Matira Beach features a mile-long strip of fine sand, flanked by palm trees and surrounded by a colorful coral reef. The beach offers the ideal backdrop for sunbathing, picnics, or just soaking in the island's calm ambiance.

The lagoons of Tahiti are a magnificent natural treasure. These enormous expanses of water are sheltered by coral reefs, giving a tranquil atmosphere for swimming, snorkeling, and other aquatic sports. The lagoons are filled with marine life, giving a paradise for underwater exploration. One of the most notable lagoons is the Rangiroa Lagoon, situated in the Tuamotu Archipelago. Known as the "Endless Lagoon," Rangiroa is the second-largest atoll in the world and is a sanctuary for snorkelers and divers. The lagoon is home to a variety of beautiful coral gardens, tropical fish, and even the rare dolphin or manta rays.

Tahiti's coral reefs are a kaleidoscope of bright hues and a home for marine species. These living structures constitute a natural barrier, preserving the lagoons and offering refuge for a diverse diversity of marine creatures. The Fakarava Atoll, a UNESCO Biosphere Reserve, is a must-visit for diving lovers. Its beautiful coral reef is home to an astounding assortment of marine life, including sharks, turtles, and schools of colorful fish. Divers may explore magnificent drop-offs, and underwater tunnels, and even swim with beautiful manta rays.

When it comes to water sports, Tahiti provides a plethora of possibilities to suit every interest and experience level. Snorkeling is a popular activity, enabling tourists to enjoy the underwater splendor of the coral reefs without the need for diving gear. Whether it's a guided trip or a solo investigation, snorkeling in Tahiti allows discovering vivid coral formations, tropical fish, and other intriguing aquatic species.

For those wanting a more immersed experience, scuba diving in Tahiti is an essential must. The island is surrounded by diving spots catering to all levels of competence. From beginner-friendly spots with calm seas and modest depths to exhilarating drift dives and deep-sea encounters,

Tahiti offers something for everyone. Divers may explore underwater tunnels, see sharks, rays, and dolphins, and view the pure splendor of the coral reefs up close.

In addition to snorkeling and diving, Tahiti also provides a choice of boating sports. From relaxing excursions around the coastline to exhilarating speedboat rides, guests may explore the lagoons and appreciate the island's beautiful splendor from the sea. Sailing aficionados may charter a sailboat or join a sailing excursion, enabling them to traverse the turquoise seas and find secret harbors and isolated beaches.

Beyond its magnificent coasts, Tahiti is also home to lush jungles, interesting hiking routes, and natural monuments. The heart of the island is a lush paradise, characterized by thick tropical woods, flowing waterfalls, and towering mountains. One famous sight is the Fautaua Valley, situated near Papeete, the capital of Tahiti. This gorgeous valley is famed for its rich greenery, cliffs, and a spectacular 985-foot waterfall. Hiking routes crisscross over the valley, affording stunning vistas and the opportunity to meet rare flora and species.

Another natural marvel of Tahiti is Mount Orohena, the highest mountain in French Polynesia. Adventure enthusiasts may go on a hard walk to the peak, traveling through steep terrain, old forests, and stunning landscapes. The wonderful panoramic views from the summit make the hike well worth the effort.

Tahiti is also peppered with several natural sites that exhibit the island's distinctive geological characteristics. One such site is the Arahoho Blowhole, situated on the northeastern shore. This natural occurrence happens when heavy waves smash against the cliffs, generating a spout of water that shoots high into the air. Visitors may watch this magnificent show of nature's fury and wonder at the sheer strength of the ocean.

In conclusion, Tahiti's gorgeous beaches, lagoons, and coral reefs offer a unique background for a variety of aquatic sports, including snorkeling, diving, and boating. The island's rich jungles, hiking paths, and natural features give a compelling contrast to its coastal splendor. Whether you're an explorer, nature lover, or just seeking leisure, Tahiti is a tropical paradise that guarantees an amazing experience.

Chapter 5

Immersing in Tahitian Culture

Polynesian culture is rich in tradition, history, and a profound connection to the land and water. Exploring the native way of life in Tahiti and immersing yourself in traditional Polynesian culture may be a genuinely enlightening experience. Let's go into some comprehensive insights into the traditional Polynesian culture and the local way of life in Tahiti, along with tips for attending cultural events, touring historical places, and connecting with local art.

The traditional Polynesian culture is profoundly anchored in the ideals of respect, community, and harmony with nature. The inhabitants of Tahiti, known as Tahitians, have kept many components of their cultural history, from their language, dance, and music to their handicrafts and storytelling.

Attending cultural events and festivals is a terrific opportunity to experience the vitality and beauty of Polynesian customs. One such event is Heiva, a month-long festival held annually in July. Heiva displays several facets of Polynesian culture, including traditional dances, music, athletic activities, and artisanal products. It's a bright and boisterous celebration that looks like the enthusiasm and passion of Tahitian culture.

In addition to Heiva, various cultural events and festivals take place throughout the year. The Tiurai Festival, held in June, offers cultural events, canoe races, and displays of traditional arts and crafts. The Tahiti Pearl Regatta mixes sailing and cultural activities, reflecting the rich maritime traditions of the area.

Traditional rituals are a vital component of Polynesian culture, and attending one may reveal significant insights into the native way of life. The "Marae" is a holy site where rites and rituals take place, signifying the link between the spiritual and physical worlds. Some marae locations, like the Marae Arahurahu, are available to tourists and provide guided tours to learn about the history and importance of these holy areas.

To better discover the historical and cultural history of Tahiti, visiting historical places is highly advised. One such place is the Pointe Vénus, where Captain James Cook first landed in Tahiti in 1769. This historical monument looks into the island's colonial history and provides a wonderful seaside backdrop for a leisurely walk or picnic.

The Museum of Tahiti and Her Islands is a must-visit for anyone interested in diving further into the island's history, ethnography, and natural sciences. The museum includes relics, exhibits, and interactive displays that offer light on the Polynesian way of life, traditional crafts, and the natural environment of French Polynesia.

To understand the creative representations of Tahitian culture, browsing art galleries is a fascinating experience. The Paul Gauguin Museum, devoted to the great French artist who found inspiration in Tahiti, displays a large collection of his works together with insights into his life on the island. The Robert Wan Pearl Museum is another unusual attraction, presenting a fascinating trip into the world of Tahitian pearls, their production, and their importance in Polynesian culture.

Engaging with local artists and craftspeople is another fantastic way to enjoy Tahitian craftsmanship. From elaborate woodcarvings and tapa cloth paintings to gorgeous pearl jewelry and traditional tattoos, the skill of the indigenous artists is extraordinary. Visiting local craft fairs and enrolling in workshops may give direct insights into traditional art forms and provide a chance to support local artists.

Overall, immersing oneself in the traditional Polynesian culture and the native way of life in Tahiti may be a changing experience. Attending cultural events, festivals, and traditional rites, touring historical monuments and museums, and interacting with local art and handicraft are all good routes to get insights into the rich legacy and dynamic spirit of Tahitian culture.

Chapter 6

Experiencing Tahitian Cuisine

Tahitian cuisine is a delicious combination of tastes, inspired by Polynesian, French, and Asian culinary traditions. The native gastronomy reflects the richness of fresh fish, tropical fruits, and root vegetables prevalent in the area. Embarking on a gastronomic trip in Tahiti means indulging in a range of unusual and tasty foods. Let's go into a thorough introduction to Tahitian food, popular local dishes, advice for sampling traditional specialties, eating at local restaurants, and visiting the finest sites to sample Tahitian cuisine and local markets.

Tahitian cuisine concentrates on fresh and locally obtained foods, emphasizing the natural tastes and simplicity of preparation. Seafood takes center stage in many recipes since the waterways around the islands teem with a diversity of fish and shellfish. Poisson cru, widely called the national dish of Tahiti, is a must-try delicacy. It comprises of raw fish marinated in lime juice and coconut milk, served with a bright variety of veggies including cucumber, tomato, and onion. The blend of citrus and creamy coconut offers a pleasant and tangy taste.

Another notable food is Fafa, a typical Polynesian dish made of taro leaves cooked in coconut milk. It's commonly served with meat, such as pig or chicken, and seasoned with indigenous herbs and spices. The taro leaves give the meal a characteristic earthy taste and a somewhat creamy texture.

Tahitian cuisine also contains a variety of dishes created using tropical fruits. One famous example is E'ia Ota, a refreshing salad prepared with chopped raw fish, lime juice, coconut milk, and a combination of tropical fruits including mango, pineapple, and papaya. The mix of the acidic fish and the sweetness of the fruits produces a perfect balance of tastes.

For those who appreciate grilled foods, Tahitian barbeque, known as Ahima'a, is a must-try experience. It includes slow-cooking meat, generally pig or chicken, in a subterranean oven called a "umu." The meat is marinated in a fragrant combination of herbs and spices before being wrapped in banana leaves and set in the hot embers of the oven. The result is soft, delicious meat with a smokey scent.

To properly experience the uniqueness of Tahitian food, touring local eateries is strongly advised. The capital city of Papeete is a gastronomic hotspot, providing a broad selection of eating alternatives that appeal to all interests and budgets. Le Coco's Restaurant is a popular option, noted for its traditional Tahitian meals and waterfront location. Here, you may experience specialties like Poisson cru, Fafa, and Ahima'a, presented with a contemporary touch.

For a superb dining experience, the Villa Mahana in Bora Bora is famous for its innovative combination of French and Tahitian cuisine. This tiny restaurant serves carefully crafted cuisine employing local ingredients, offering a fascinating gastronomic adventure.

Exploring local markets is also a terrific opportunity to explore Tahitian food. The Papeete Market, also known as Le Marché de Papeete, is a lively marketplace where you can discover an abundance of fresh food, spices, and traditional crafts. It's a wonderful spot to enjoy tropical fruits, local delicacies, and handmade preserves. The market also has food kiosks where you can sar in local delights including Poisson cru, coconut bread, and freshly squeezed fruit juices.

If you're visiting Moorea, the Moorea Tropical Garden and Fruit Juice Factory is a terrific site to explore. This botanical park not only provides a spectacular display of tropical flora but also shows traditional fruit farming techniques. You may experience a broad selection of freshly squeezed fruit juices, including unusual flavors like guava, passion fruit, and soursop.

In conclusion, Tahitian cuisine provides a delightful combination of tastes, merging native ingredients with influences from Polynesian, French, and Asian culinary traditions. Trying traditional specialties like Poisson cru, Fafa, and Ahima'a is a necessity for a genuine Tahitian dining experience. Dining at local restaurants, such as Le Coco's Restaurant or Villa Mahana, enables you to experience the creativity and competence of local chefs. Exploring marketplaces like the Papeete Market and the Moorea Tropical Garden allows the opportunity to try tropical fruits, native foods, and freshly squeezed juices. Embarking on a gastronomic trip around Tahiti is guaranteed to please your taste senses and expose you to the colorful tastes of this beautiful resort.

Chapter 7

Practical Tips and Safety

When arranging a vacation to Tahiti, it's crucial to be prepared and knowledgeable to guarantee a seamless and pleasurable experience. Here are some extensive travel instructions including packing ideas, what to wear, safety precautions, managing funds, currency conversion, and communication choices while in Tahiti.

Packing tips for Tahiti should concentrate on the tropical climate and the island's laid-back attitude. Here are some crucial factors to consider:

Lightweight and breathable clothing: Pack loose-fitting garments made from natural fibers like cotton and linen to keep comfortable in the warm and humid atmosphere. Don't forget to pack swimsuits, cover-ups, and a cap to protect yourself from the sun.

Sun protection: Tahiti sees intense sun rays, so make sure to take sunscreen with a high SPF, sunglasses, and a sunhat to safeguard yourself from dangerous UV rays.

Insect repellent: Although Tahiti doesn't have a large mosquito issue, it's always a good idea to pack insect repellent to prevent bites, particularly if you intend on spending time in the evenings outside or exploring the lush woods.

Snorkeling gear: If you intend on snorkeling, consider bringing your snorkel mask and fins for a more customized experience. However, most hotels and tour companies offer snorkeling gear for hire.

prescriptions and essentials: Pack any required prescription prescriptions in their original containers, along with a basic first-aid kit that contains band-aids, disinfectant, and other personal medications you may need. Also, consider packing motion sickness medicine if you're prone to seasickness.

Safety recommendations and measures are crucial to guarantee a safe and pleasurable journey to Tahiti. Here are some crucial considerations to keep in mind:

Water safety: While the seas of Tahiti are typically safe, it's always good to use care while swimming or partaking in water sports. Pay heed to any safety warnings or advice issued by local authorities and travel providers. Additionally, be careful of possible strong currents and carry a life jacket when required.

Protect your stuff: Tahiti is a secure place, but it's still vital to take care to preserve your valuables. Use hotel safes to secure your valuables, keep a watch on your possessions in public locations, and avoid flaunting costly goods or huge sums of cash.

Respect local customs: Tahitian culture lays a high focus on respect and humility. When visiting holy locations, such as marae, dress properly and observe any recommendations or prohibitions. It's also usual to remove your shoes before entering someone's house or a traditional institution.

remain hydrated: Tahiti's tropical environment may be hot and humid, so it's vital to remain hydrated. Carry a refillable water bottle and drink lots of water throughout the day, particularly if you're spending time outside or engaging in activities.

Managing funds, currency exchange, and communication choices in Tahiti:

Currency: The official currency of French Polynesia is the French Pacific Franc (XPF). It's good to keep some local cash on hand for modest transactions and in more distant places. Major credit cards are frequently accepted at hotels, restaurants, and bigger institutions. ATMs are present in towns and cities for cash withdrawals.

Communication: Tahiti has a solid telecommunications infrastructure, and you should have access to mobile network service in most regions. Check with your mobile service provider to confirm your phone has international roaming enabled. Alternatively, you may acquire a local SIM card for your unlocked phone upon arrival.

Language: The official languages of Tahiti are French and Tahitian. English is also spoken in tourist areas, however, it's essential to learn a few basic Tahitian phrases to show respect and interact with the people.

Internet access: Most hotels, resorts, and cafés provide Wi-Fi for guests. If you require a continual internet connection, consider getting a local SIM card with data for your mobile device.

Budgeting: Tahiti may be an expensive vacation, so it's wise to arrange your money properly. Research the usual expenditures of rooms, food, activities, and transportation to get a realistic picture of your spending. Consider reserving packages or all-inclusive choices to ease budgeting.

In conclusion, being prepared with suitable attire, following safety requirements, managing funds, and ensuring communication alternatives are vital for a comfortable and pleasurable vacation to Tahiti. By packing sensibly, remaining knowledgeable about safety concerns, managing your funds properly, and preserving communication options, you can completely immerse yourself in the beauty and culture of Tahiti while having a worry-free holiday.

Printed in Great Britain
by Amazon

39596425R00030